The Mighty World of

TRUCKS

The Mighty World of

TRUCKS

FOG
CITY

PRESS

Published by Fog City Press,
a division of Weldon Owen Inc.
1045 Sansome Street
San Francisco, CA 94111 USA

www.weldonowen.com

weldon**owen**
President & Publisher Roger Shaw
Associate Publisher Mariah Bear
SVP, Sales & Marketing Amy Kaneko
Finance Manager Philip Paulick
Editor Bridget Fitzgerald
Creative Director Kelly Booth
Art Director Meghan Hildebrand
Senior Production Designer Rachel Lopez Metzger
Production Director Chris Hemesath
Associate Production Director Michelle Duggan
Director of Enterprise Systems Shawn Macey
Imaging Manager Don Hill

Library of Congress Control Number on file with the publisher.

ISBN 13: 978-1-68188-097-6
ISBN 10: 1-68188-097-0

10 9 8 7 6 5 4 3 2 1

2016 2017 2018 2019

Printed by 1010 Printing in China.

Day or night, trucks never stop working, carrying all the things we need in our daily lives.

Trucks take our food from farmers and factories to supermarkets. They plow snow in winter, work on construction sites, and help build houses. They clear away garbage to keep our world clean.

You can see trucks being busy all around you. Keep an eye out for some of these mighty machines.

Trucks come in all kinds of shapes, sizes, and colors.

FUN FACT
"Big rigs" are huge trucks with lots of wheels.

The front part of a truck is called a tractor. The tractor pulls the trailer along behind.

FUN FACT
The tractor-trailer was invented over 100 years ago.

FUN FACT
Big rigs can weigh
as much as 20 or
30 cars!

Trucks are built to travel long distances,
from sunny deserts to snowy mountains.

FUN FACT
Some trucks go on drives that take many months.

The driver sits in the cab. Drivers can stop and rest in a little room at the back if they get tired.

The cab has lights, horns, and shiny exhaust pipes. Without its trailer, the tractor looks very bare.

FUN FACT
Removable gooseneck trailers can haul very tall loads.

Trailers are loaded using a forklift. Sometimes the forklift drives straight up the ramp.

FUN FACT
The kingpin is the pin that connects the tractor and trailer.

FUN FACT
Trucks are sorted by how much weight they can carry.

Some trailers are loaded with goods straight from a factory or warehouse.

Have you seen trucks on busy highways? When you see an empty truck you know it's on the way to get a new load.

FUN FACT
A semi-trailer has wheels only on the rear end.

FUN FACT

Tanks come in many sizes. Some are even refrigerated!

These big
trucks are
called tank
trucks. Their
long trailers
carry liquids
like milk or oil.

These trucks are at the docks, picking up loads of goods that have come from another country.

FUN FACT
These huge metal containers attach to the trailers.

FUN FACT
Road trains are some of the biggest trucks anywhere!

Road trains are huge trucks that haul lots
of trailers at once. They are common
on the long roads in Australia.

FUN FACT
Some people drive pickup trucks instead of cars.

A pickup or a small cargo truck is handy for carrying a small load or just cruising around town.

Tow trucks rescue cars that have broken down and take them away.

FUN FACT
Tow trucks are sometimes called draggin' wagons!

FUN FACT
Look for garbage trucks driving around early in the morning!

Garbage trucks take away trash. Street sweepers clean our roads.

Dump trucks
carry soil, sand,
and gravel at
building sites.

FUN FACT
The back of the dump truck is a tray that tilts to tip the load.

FUN FACT
These massive trucks are also used for mining.

Construction workers use dump trucks to move materials such as dirt, gravel, and sand.

These loggers are transporting trees. The wood will be turned into paper and new furniture.

FUN FACT

Iron bars on the sides of the trucks prevent falling logs.

Cement-mixers mix cement and water to make
concrete. Their drums are always turning in
order to keep the concrete from getting hard!

FUN FACT
Cement truck drums contain sharp blades to mix the concrete.

FUN FACT
Snowplows move piles of snow, like bulldozers push around dirt.

Snowplows work hard in the winter, clearing snow from the roads.

Monster trucks like to show off—they crush cars, jump in the air, and perform tricks!

FUN FACT
Monster trucks can star in shows called rallies.

Key: SS=Shutterstock; iSP=iStockphoto; t=top; b=bottom;